Beacon of Hope

NEW BEACON IN
POETRY AND PROSE

Beacon of Hope

New Beacon Books

George Padmore Institute

Published 2016 by New Beacon Books Ltd., 76 Stroud Green Road, London N4 3EN for the George Padmore Institute

© 2016 Jay Bernard for 'Surge'

© 2013 Ruth Bush for 'New Beacon Books the Pioneering Years' Originally published online as part of the HLF funded *Dream To Change The World Project*. Published in this form 2016.

ISBN 978 1 873201 33 6

Page 58, illustration by Jay Bernard

All other illustrations courtesy the George Padmore Institute archives

Printed by Imprint Digital, Exeter, England

Contents

Preface

The George Padmore Institute is publishing this commemorative book on the occasion of the 50th Anniversary of New Beacon Books founded, originally as a publisher, in 1966. *Beacon of Hope: New Beacon in Poetry and Prose* contains creative work and research recently carried out under the auspices of the GPI. The Institute was set up in 1991 by New Beacon Books. It contains archives that have a unique activist and organic character arising from the independent cultural, educational and political activity of the group of people and organisations centred around the GPI and New Beacon.

'**New Beacon Books – the pioneering years**', by Ruth Bush, is the online essay that she researched and wrote as part of the five year HLF funded 'Dream to Change the World Project' [2010-2015]. Since its launch in 2014, there have been requests to make it also available as a printed version. We thought that including it in this volume would be a very apt contribution to New Beacon's 50th Anniversary Celebrations.

At the heart of these celebrations, organised by the George Padmore Institute, was the appointment of a poet-in-residence. Black British poet, Jay Bernard, has spent three months exploring the GPI's archives, including the recently catalogued personal papers of John La Rose. Her poem, creatively reflecting on her experience, is here published under the title **'Surge'**.

The title for the book comes from Linton Kwesi Johnson's poem 'Beacon of Hope'.

from Beacon of Hope

(for John La Rose)

...

tonight you will illuminate the path of dreams
Like glow-worms of the northern climes
your flashing fluorescence
are eyes of light
flashing sparks
that pierce the dark
of my moonless starless tropical night

welcome nocturnal friend
I name you beacon of hope
...

Linton Kwesi Johnson, *Selected Poems*
Penguin, 2006, p. 62

New Beacon Books – the Pioneering Years

RUTH BUSH

Sarah White and John La Rose in New Beacon Books.

Archive ref. GB 2904 LRA/5 (uncatalogued)

New Beacon Books – the Pioneering Years

New Beacon early history

Founded in 1966 by John La Rose and Sarah White, New Beacon Books emerged from a swell of radical ideas and actions. It became a bookshop, an international book service and a community hub, as well as the first independent publisher for Caribbean and black interest fiction and non-fiction in the UK.

This essay sets out New Beacon's publishing achievements during its first ten years using material from the recently catalogued archive of its founder, John La Rose. These archives are held at New Beacon's sister organisation, the George Padmore Institute. The aim is to trace New Beacon's history in relation to the emergence of an independent radical black publishing space in Britain in the late 1960s and 1970s.

The essay sketches the background against which New Beacon arrived on the British and Caribbean publishing scene, indicating material from the archive which may spark further research. We will consider both what was published and what was not published in New Beacon's eclectic catalogue of poetry, non-fiction, reprinted classics, short histories and critical writing.

Why write this history of publishing?

A publisher's task is to transform a handwritten or typed manuscript into a printed or electronic book, taking the text from its author to the shelves of a bookshop or online retailer. The process involves selecting what to publish; editing and designing the book; the logistics of marketing, rights, royalties and sales. An underlying consideration therefore is how the history of New Beacon's publishing fits with wider political and cultural shifts in book production as a form of political resistance. This analysis acknowledges that while in the late twentieth and early twenty-first centuries book publishing has rapidly been outpaced in the political sphere by other forms of media, questions of access to printed information and freedom of expression remain vital.

Publishing is never neutral or value-free. Even as the book industry undergoes huge changes in the digital era, publishing demands a combination of creative input, decision-making and dedication to the practical administrative tasks. New Beacon has played an important, if under-acknowledged, role in the gradual social and cultural diversification of knowledge production in Britain. Building on the exemplary, in-depth work of Anne Walmsley (1992) and Brian Alleyne (2002), the present study is intended less as a monument to the passing of a certain mode of independent publishing or to the ebbs and flows of radical black political ideas, than as a balanced discussion of the short and long-term achievements of New Beacon Books.

Amid the maelstrom of black consciousness movements, progressive left-wing politics, Cold War tensions and the rise of Third Worldism, New Beacon represented a challenge to the status quo of the British publishing field, offering new means for selecting, channelling and circulating information. Alongside other publishers, including Bogle-L'Ouverture, Allison & Busby and the Race Today Collective in Britain, Présence Africaine and Editions Maspero in France, *New World Quarterly*, *Tapia* and *Savacou* in the Caribbean, and Third World Press in the USA, New Beacon forged a resilient space for independent radical black publishing. This early period culminated in the success of the International Book Fair of Radical Black and Third World Booksellers, which was held annually from 1982 to 1995 (White et al).

John La Rose's presence as a federating figure and voice of experience and encouragement, together with the central role played by Sarah White, depended on human relationships built through trust and a firm belief in the social, cultural and political value of communicating ideas at local and global levels. Faced with the challenges of a colonial legacy and his chosen exile to Britain, La Rose saw publishing as a means to ensure continuity over distance and time. Ten years after New Beacon was founded, he described the project in an interview as:

> A vehicle which gave an independent validation of one's own culture, history, politics – a sense of one's self – to break the discontinuity. It can't be done totally because we are not in control of the schools, we don't have control of the media, we are not in control of everything that impinges on a person's life in the society. However, you can break some elements of that discontinuity and give people some sense of what is important, so that they get some sense of what they need to know to transform their lives. (*Race Today* interview, June/July 1977, 82-84)

Publishing can be radical since it affects the fundamental ways in which information is selected, packaged and circulated in print. The word 'radical' itself comes from the Latin *radicalis*: relating to or forming the root. The widespread radical reform of rooted social or political ideas depends on intellectual insight, thorough commitment and long-term hard work, qualities which together characterise the history of radical black publishing in Britain.

At a time when publishing is undergoing seismic shifts and uncertainty reigns over its future form as an industry, the record of this history reminds us of the complex human networks and the social, political and economic forces that shaped the production of the written word in the last century. As such, it is a key aspect of Black British history and of media history more widely. It reminds us that writing (and reading) does not occur in a vacuum, encouraging us to question critically how texts are shaped by the contexts in which they are produced. Tracing the often-concealed context of production suggests new layers of meaning, as well as alerting us to the contingency of our own reading experiences. In the case of Caribbean and black diasporic writing, it raises important questions: How did editors located in the former colonial centre choose what, and what not, to publish? How did they then produce and distribute that writing? What might the choice of binding (soft or hardback) tell us about a book's intended readers? How do the illustrations and book covers work towards, or against, certain notions of Caribbean/black identity?

Why publish independently?
To answer this question, a fuller understanding of black writing in the post-war book market in Britain and the Caribbean is necessary. As has been well-documented, a number of foundational figures in Caribbean literature published their first books in Britain in the late 1940s and 1950s. The decline of the British Empire, the rise of anti-colonial independence movements and the 'Windrush' generation of migration from the Caribbean to Britain in the late 1940s, were accompanied by a rise in interest in cultural expression from the colonised regions. Such interest continued, to a large extent, to be filtered through metropolitan institutions that selected, produced, distributed and funded literature in the post-war period. These included commercial, scholarly and established literary publishing houses: Oxford University Press, Longman, Heinemann, Hutchinson, André Deutsch, Jonathan Cape, Faber & Faber and others. Gail Low describes this unprecedented interest on the part of British publishers and their readership as a combination of

'curiosity, concern, exoticism and opportunism' (xiv). Authors in the 'boom' included Sam Selvon, George Lamming, Andrew Salkey, Wilson Harris, Derek Walcott, John Hearne, Edgar Mittelholzer and V.S. Naipaul, all of whom, except Derek Walcott, also relocated physically to London in this period. Diana Athill, V.S. Naipaul's editor at André Deutsch, goes so far as to suggest that in the 1950s and early 60s, it was probably easier for a young black writer to get his book accepted by a London publisher than it was for a young white person (Athill, 102). Further research remains to be done on the ways in which writing by Caribbean writers was edited, selected and packaged during the 1950s and early 1960s by mainstream publishers. Such work could explore further the complex structural relationships between political changes reflected in immigration policies, the position of Caribbean writing in the publishing field and the emergence of black British literary traditions.

Many of the London and Caribbean-based writers benefited from the weekly *Caribbean Voices* radio programme, founded by the Jamaican poet and journalist Una Marson in 1943 and subsequently edited by Henry Swanzy from 1946 to 1958, then briefly by V.S. Naipaul. *Caribbean Voices* helped circulate the work of young Caribbean writers and nurture a literary culture and network of writers. Henry Swanzy provided an informal kind of literary mentorship, but also arguably promoted writing which reflected his preference for narratives of 'local colour' (Low, 102). Gerald Moore has written of the parallel role played by the BBC Transcription Centre in the sixties as a meeting place and broadcaster for African writers visiting London. One of New Beacon's early publications, *Caribbean Writers: critical essays*, was based on programmes broadcast by the Transcription Centre, confirming the importance of radio broadcasting in Caribbean literary production. Several critics have described and analysed the significance of this context of exile in creating a sense of regional identity (Kenneth Ramchand, C.L. Innes, James Procter). Less has been written about the institutional contexts for Caribbean writing in the late 1960s and 1970s, a period during which that regional label gained more fluid definitions, blurring into an expanding body of Black British fiction and non-fiction.

Critics have described the tensions between the regional identity and 'local colour' fostered by *Caribbean Voices* and the ostensibly universal qualities championed by London publishers (Low, 114). New Beacon's catalogue and radical black publishing space in the late 1960s and '70s challenged the institutional annexation of black literature to a eurocentric narrative of literary modernism. New Beacon moved neither in the direction of championing the universal aesthetic value of Caribbean art, nor towards that of commodifying art that packaged restrictive versions of Caribbean identity. This point is confirmed by the range of its publications in fiction and non-fiction. One of the most significant characteristics of this radical black publishing space is the juxtaposition of genres: from poetry to biography, history and political philosophy.

A major sign of this shift towards greater critical autonomy in the late sixties was the founding of the Caribbean Artists Movement (CAM) in 1966 by Jamaican novelist and journalist, Andrew Salkey, Bajan poet and doctoral student in history, L. Edward (now Kamau) Brathwaite and John La Rose. They, and like-minded writers and artists met frequently in London and organised readings, conferences and cultural events, starting with a landmark performance of Brathwaite's *Rights of Passage* at the Jeanetta Cochrane theatre in March 1967. Their aim was to foster an independent space for discussing and promoting Caribbean artistic and literary production and in turn alter the terms against which that work was to be judged and given value. Their work built on preceding examples of black cultural affirmation in the Caribbean (Cuban *negrismo* in the 1920s), the United States (the Harlem Renaissance of the 1920s) and France (the *négritude* movement of the 1930s), as reflected in the scope of their subjects for discussion. CAM meetings were the first place where La Rose and Sarah White began selling their own publications and those of other small publishers. New Beacon's bookshop thus began its life at this forum as a bag of books transported around London on Sarah White's Honda 50 motorbike.

Sarah White on her Honda 50 bike, 1964.

Archive ref. GB 2904 LRA/5 (uncatalogued)

At this point it is necessary to widen the lens to include non-fiction and educational publishing. Specialist Caribbean books were developed at Longman from 1967 (with Anne Walmsley as editor) and at Heinemann, where James Currey launched the Caribbean Writers Series in 1970 (starting with *A Year in San Fernando* by Michael Anthony). Anne Walmsley had worked as an English teacher in Jamaica for three years after four spent working as secretary at Faber and Faber in the late fifties. She joined Longman as Caribbean editor after a stint working for BBC television on her return to London. She recalls approaching several other publishers proposing herself as a Caribbean specialist editor before being offered the job at Longman over a glass of sherry in their Mayfair offices:

> They told me they wanted to appoint their first Caribbean publisher and would I be interested? 'You'll have to meet lots of new people', they said, 'and you'll have to travel to the Caribbean twice a year'. That was how I got the job, in 1967. I was sent on a 'familiarisation tour' for three months whizzing up and down the Caribbean. After that I went twice a year – and travelled with local representatives in Trinidad and Jamaica. (Interview)

Walmsley worked closely with Longman's representatives in Trinidad and Jamaica, Eastlyn Bynoe and Vivien Carrington, who subsequently managed Longman Caribbean offices on those islands. Meanwhile, in London she attended early CAM meetings through her friendship with Kamau Brathwaite and Doris Brathwaite, where she made contact with writers and first met John La Rose and Sarah White. These discussions in turn informed her work for Longman, reminding us that the independent critical space forged by CAM was an open forum for developing ideas and responses to artistic creation across lines of race, gender and social class, rather than a militant political project.

Longman played an important role in providing Caribbean specific educational material through consultation with Caribbean teachers. It expanded the space for books by black authors in the Caribbean, though it had notably little distribution in Britain. One of the main aims of New Beacon's book service was to make books by Caribbean writers about the Caribbean readily available in Britain. Larger publishers had recognised the commercial success possible through the channelling of African literature into specialised paperback series in the 1960s, notably Heinemann's African Writers Series, edited by Chinua Achebe, and OUP's Three Crown Series (Currey; Davis). Such series faced very different contexts in Africa and the Caribbean, though both encouraged new writing by providing a strong distribution network and catering for the expanding schools readership with large print-runs of economically priced paperback books. New Beacon's publishing work emerged out of this shared context, but with very different goals.

'Is we speak to we now'

New Beacon's publishing work was in part a response to the metropolitan ownership of the means of book production, though they did not envisage, at least in the short term, competing in commercial terms with Longman, Heinemann, Nelson or the other major players. New Beacon Books is what might be termed a 'micro-publisher', having published 65 books between 1966 and 2012, and John La Rose would often refer to the venture modestly as a 'publishing maisonette':

> It was never our intention to become anything but a small to medium publisher and bookseller. We knew the other political and cultural commitments that we had, and we continued to want to make, and that therefore we couldn't really think of ourselves as being full-time publishers and booksellers, in the

way that if you were going into this business as a commercial operation. (cited in Goulbourne, 153)

New Beacon retains its symbolic stature as a radical publisher in part because of this rejection of profit-making goals, which in turn allowed it to take certain risks, in line with the ethos of most small independent publishers. New Beacon and other independent black publishers marked an important symbolic shift in the publishing landscape, as seen in this letter from Kamau Brathwaite to La Rose:

> i going to cuss off oxford, yale, doubleday, longmans and a whole set o these exploiters who jess reject my white power in j'ca. them doan want we to say what we got to say. and what base not on fancy, but on dem hard hard document.

> in anycase, is we to speak to we now: that is why new beacon must survive and grow; why bogle must survive and grow; why savacou must survive and grow. (EKB to JLR 6.6 (no year), LRA/01/0143/4)

This strategy of 'we to speak to we now' encapsulates the call for new independent alternatives to the established publishing field. Most writers, including politically radical voices such as Brathwaite, continued to publish with larger publishers while turning to New Beacon for smaller projects. What is clear, however, is that by the late sixties, there was little place for the paternalistic approach of figures such as Henry Swanzy who had shaped Caribbean literary publishing in the previous decades. As Swanzy wrote in his journal after a CAM conference session where he had spoken in 1968, he was looked upon as a 'Swanzy-zombie' in the new climate (Walmsley, 167).

It might well be asked why the vast majority of books bought, borrowed or read in the English-speaking Caribbean were published in London throughout this period. Despite the strength of local press and magazine printing in the Caribbean both before and after the 'boom', this situation reflected the limited means of producing and distributing books on the islands. Increasingly, authors sought publishers who would secure a large readership for their work and provide them with regulated working conditions (consistent marketing, regular royalties etc.). Publishing in London by mainstream publishers had ongoing material benefits in this regard. For some authors being published in the British capital conferred a form of symbolic prestige. The work of ground-breaking little Caribbean magazines and other culturally-oriented journals remained strong however during the late 1960s: *Savacou* (1970-1989) was founded as part of a planned Caribbean branch of CAM (AW 202-205). Other publications included *New World Quarterly* (1963-1968), *Voices* (1964-1966), *Tapia* (1969-) and *Jamaica Journal* (1970-). Several of these publications have been digitised by the Digital Library of the Caribbean They were important publicity outlets for New Beacon's early publications and each merits further research in its own right.

New Beacon's ethos as an independent radical publisher was motivated by principles of autonomy, freedom and community, as understood in relation to global contexts of decolonisation and the Cold War which inflected local contexts of discrimination in Britain. John La Rose defended these principles of artistic freedom in a long letter to Andrew Salkey:

> The artist whose tool (production tool) is his/her imagination is uncontrollable and uncontrolled. The tool escapes the totality. (but everything else that is needed to turn the creation of the imagination into product – sculpture, book etc. is within the control). (7.1.77, JLR to AS, LRA/01/0698/1 Pt2, p10)

While acknowledging powerful forms of imaginative

resistance, La Rose was aware of other forms of power and control – here seen as part of a political 'totality' managed by the state – exerted by publishing and other institutional forms of artistic production. In the same letter, written ten years after New Beacon's founding, he referred to the Heberto Padilla affair in Cuba – the important case of a poet who had been punished after speaking out against Castro's Cuba. The comments express a certain disillusionment with post-revolutionary disregard for creative freedom:

> The relationship between culture and politics, the artist and society, cultural creativity and political creativity continue to bedevil and stretch on the rack of post-revolutionary societies [...] The state control of all resources is the source of the trouble in the bureaucratised state. The Organisation Men control the printing press, the ink, the paper for book production, journal production, distribution, access to books to travel to people. (7.1.77, JLR to AS, LRA/01/0698/1 Pt2)

While New Beacon's 'dream to change the world' can be described as utopian, the letter reminds us of La Rose's alertness to the potential forms of control that exist either side of revolution. For radical independent publishers in Britain, the decision to publish or not to publish remained contingent on practical issues of financial means. Their greater freedom at the stage of selection and production faced challenges of distribution and sales. In the case of New Beacon Books and CAM, this meant a tension between their political aims to create an enabling form of autonomy and open possibilities for more fluid and creative notions of identity, and the ongoing monopoly of the Caribbean book market by large publishing houses. As Brian Alleyne writes, New Beacon's activism is 'not only built around resistance, but seeks actively to create alternative systems of value and communication' (2).

The beginnings of New Beacon Books

The idea of founding a publishing house had been in gestation since the early years of John La Rose's political activism in Trinidad and Venezuela. La Rose was born in Arima, Trinidad in 1927 where his father was a cocoa trader and his mother a teacher. He won a scholarship to St Mary's College, Port of Spain, and became an insurance executive after leaving school. He was active in the Workers Freedom Movement in the 1940s as editor of their journal, and a trade union activist, particularly in the Oilfield Workers Trade Union. During this period he became acquainted with Marxist thought, through the guidance of older colleagues Neville Giuseppi and Arnold Thomasos (Gus John). As the struggle for independence heightened, La Rose helped found the West Indian Independence Party in 1956 and stood (unsuccessfully) in that year's general election. In 1958 he moved to Venezuela to escape from the discrimination he experienced in Trinidad because of his political activism. He arrived in Britain in 1961, intending to study Law before returning to the Caribbean to continue the struggle to secure the region's future.

By this point he had already published widely in Caribbean newspapers and magazines and had co-authored a book on Kaiso with the great Calypsonian Raymond Quevedo (re-published in Trinidad in 1983 as *Atilla's Kaiso*). La Rose's first wife, Irma, and two sons Michael and Keith moved to London shortly after this date. John La Rose continued to campaign as

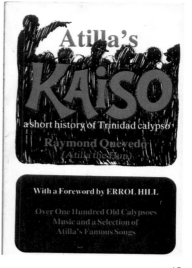

European representative of the Oilfields Workers Trade Union and became fully committed to the idea of founding a publishing house after meeting Sarah White, Andrew Salkey and Kamau Brathwaite.

Publishing required more than a good idea and some willpower: as for any business, a certain amount of money would also be required. After abandoning his legal studies, John La Rose worked variously as an agricultural labourer, a hotel porter, in the canteen at Selfridges and as a bricklayer on a site by Moorgate Station in central London. During the latter job he became active as shop steward for the building trade union. He enjoyed the work and built on his wealth of experience in the labour movement in the Caribbean. This experience informs a poem in La Rose's first volume of poetry, published by New Beacon ('On the site') which celebrates the comradeship among members of the building trade union.

On the same day that Nkrumah was deposed in Ghana (24 February 1966), La Rose suffered an accident on site, falling from a weak scaffold and injuring his back. He was well placed to pursue a successful claim against his employers and published New Beacon's first book with a few hundred pounds as a direct result of this payout. The first publication was *Foundations*, La Rose's first volume of poetry. This was soon followed by a collection of essays by Wilson Harris, *Tradition, the Writer and Society* and a short biography of Marcus Garvey by Adolph Edwards. The company was registered as a private limited company on 1 August 1967 with La Rose and Sarah White as equal share-holders. It was named after *The Beacon*, a ground-breaking journal and literary group formed by C.L.R. James, Albert Gomes and Alfred Mendes in the early 1930s in Trinidad.

Sarah White grew up in West Hampstead and attended school in Bristol. Her mother, Edith Dorothy (known as Dodo) came from a Newcastle ship-engineering family and after the war was politically active as a secretary with the local Liberal Party in Hampstead. Her father, Eric Walter White, was involved in the Council for the Encouragement of Music and the Arts (CEMA) during the war and later joined the newly formed Arts Council. He later became its first Literature Director. Sarah White attended Leeds University, initially to study Chemistry, but switched to History of Science and Russian after her first term. This interest stemmed from a period spent learning Russian between A levels and university after a summer holiday in Yugoslavia. White's political activism began at university, where she joined the Communist Party and became involved in local campaigns in Yorkshire and the anti-Apartheid campaign. After university she spent a year in Moscow on a course for teachers of Russian as a foreign language. She recalls her changing attitude to Communism during that period:

> The thing about the Communist Party, it was well-organised, it gave you a sort of structure to be active on, but it was very prescriptive in the sense of, you know, *this* was the right line or *that* was the right line, rather than exploring ideas. And I always remember, I got to Moscow for that year, which was really interesting. That was 63/64. I remember going to schools, because we did a lot, we went into schools, we went all over the place, we used to go to the theatre a lot, and listen to the teachers talking to the kids, and teaching in a way that there was only one answer. It was quite interesting. At the same time, they were so much better educated than us! (Interview)

On her return to London, White decided to undertake a PhD at Imperial College on the reception of Darwinism in Russia while living with her parents in Islington. It was during this time that she became involved with organising an anti-colonial exhibition and doing voluntary work for the African National Congress (ANC) at the Africa Centre, located round the corner from the West Indian Students'

Centre. Both Centres were the base for anti-colonial movements in Britain. It was here that White first met La Rose, at a meeting where Paule Marshall was speaking, and after having read the *West Indians' Bulletin* that he edited:

> He was there and we were introduced, and I thought 'Oh, what a lovely smile' [...] He'd sent this West Indian newsletter or whatever it was called. *West Indians' Bulletin* [...] this thing arrived at the house and I was looking at it and I couldn't quite make it out. Because you know, when you're in the Communist Party [...] things have a line, they have a particular line, and if you're a Trotskyist they have another line. And never two lines shall meet. But, I was looking at this thing, and it was radical, sort of seemed Marxist and all the rest of it, but it didn't follow a line, so I was slightly intrigued by it. And I didn't know quite how I'd got onto this mailing list so then I met him and discovered he was the person doing it! But then where we really met properly was when the Americans invaded the Dominican Republic and a small committee was set up, and, this is 65 we're talking about, and we both landed up on the committee. That's how it all took off.

After defending her thesis successfully, White began work at the *New Scientist* as a science journalist from 1967. This helped fund the work of New Beacon and family life with a regular income. Her and John's son, Wole, was born in 1969, and White continued her journalism on a part-time basis until the early '80s, alongside her commitments to the publishing house and the book service. She still works full-time for New Beacon today and is a trustee of the George Padmore Institute.

Race, class, and politics: the intertwining contexts
New Beacon Books was both a symptom and an outcome of shifts in the intertwined politics of race, class and black culture in Britain during the late 1960s. As has been well-

documented, post-war immigration from the Caribbean provided labour to secure Britain's post-war recovery. Successive waves of immigration following the first 'Windrush' generation of the late forties led gradually to an expanded black population, though there had been a settled black population in Britain for much longer than this (Fryer; Adim-Ado; and other historians). Housing and education were often difficult, as newcomers faced challenging realities of discrimination. In response, the late fifties saw riots in Notting Hill and the formation of the West Indian Standing Conference, which campaigned for certain rights, while many black people also sought to join existing political parties and organised labour movements.

John La Rose had moved to Britain just before the 1962 Immigration Act which placed strict limits on levels of immigration. In the latter half of the decade black political activity became increasingly militant and organised in response to increasingly widespread racial discrimination, combined with a lack of government response to that situation (Phillips). Groups such as Michael X's Racial Action Adjustment Society and the Universal Coloured People's Association organised protests. The sense of potential transformation was bolstered by visits to Britain of Malcolm X in 1965 and Stokely Carmichael in 1967 and the media noise surrounding the Black Panthers (Phillips, 223-241). These movements were related in complex ways to the rising strength of radical student politics internationally: Maoism, Trotskyism, international socialism and reactions to the Cold War context, which came to a symbolic head in the student protests of May 1968. These events reverberate through the archives at the George Padmore Institute as ongoing discussion traced how political change and instability reverberated and met new responses in the post-independence, English-speaking Caribbean. Writer and teacher Merle Hodge described her students in Trinidad as 'effervescent & self-opinionated to a degree that we never dreamt of, and seething with protest' (MH to JLR, 8.4.71, LRA/01/0386). In Guyana there were rebellions against the government of Forbes Burnham. In London, John La Rose, Eric and Jessica Huntley and many others who had been politically active in the Caribbean before moving to Britain were involved in protests and organised the important 1965 Guyana Symposium in response. Elsewhere Jamaica was hit by protests following the government's banning of Walter Rodney in 1968 on charges of sedition, while Trinidad faced widespread unrest in 1970-1971, triggered by arrests of West Indian students at a Canadian university (See Walmsley, 217).

In Britain, Enoch Powell's incendiary 'Rivers of Blood' speech on 20 April 1968 epitomised a racist rhetoric that set the tone for the new British Conservative government of 1970. During the following decade's economic recession, their policies included a series of Immigration and Race Relations Acts that imposed new legally sanctioned discrimination. Ambalavaner Sivanandan, writer and director of the Institute of Race Relations, writes of the changes that took place in the 1970s:

> The race scene was changing – radically. The Immigration Acts, whatever their racialist promptings, had stemmed from an economic rationale, fashioned in the matrix of colonial-capitalist practices and beliefs. They served, as we have seen, to take racial discrimination out of the market-place and institutionalise it – inhere it in the structures of the state, locally and nationally. So that at both local and national levels 'race' became an area of contestation for power. (18)

Throughout the post-war period, the relationship between black politics and the established left-wing political class in Britain was uncertain, facing moments of conflict and consensus. These tensions continued unabated through the 1970s and into the 1980s (Gilroy, 1987; 2002). Brian Alleyne writes that:

> The framework within which the ideas and work of the New Beacon circle should be placed initially is one where relationships between anti-racist and left/radical politics in Britain were built, a space where the classic Old Left met the New Left and the different tendencies of Black radicalism which arose in the wake of Black Power. (30)

La Rose was aware of the lived complexity of race and class in the radical politics of the period through his involvement in local community activism. He was also particularly attuned to the international co-ordinates of often contradictory political positions in Britain. He wrote to Kamau Brathwaite, describing the London scene:

> The Trotskyists and Communists and other assorted left are making a bid to behead the Black Peoples Movement. It's all becoming very clear over the solidarity movement with Angela Davis and The Soledad Brothers and the mass meeting of solidarity with Amilcar Cabral and Guinea Bissau. It's like what happened with Steelband in a different context. They will march about Vietnam and everything else, but what happens here to Black people is too close to the bone. The Mangrove 9 is not seen as what it is – police terror against Black people because our resistance is to the whole society. (JLR to EKB 24.10.71, LRA/01/0143/4)

As the decade progressed, the anti-war and women's liberation movements provided contexts in which local activism expanded, though the fault lines between these radical principles were rarely straightforward. Brian Alleyne writes:

> That many people know New Beacon only or mainly as a 'Black Bookshop' is indicative of the reductionist way in which everyday as well as sociological understanding of radical

political activity involving any significant number of Black people is often transformed into 'Black politics' and the radical element is jettisoned. (41)

La Rose was consistently opposed to exclusive forms of black nationalism and saw New Beacon's work as part of a fundamental (that is, *radical*) change in the organisation of society and culture. Black consciousness movements, such as Black Power and Rastafarianism, together with Marxist ideas fed into his thinking. His humanist orientation was sympathetic to the work of these different currents, without aligning itself totally with any single ideology. He wrote to Andrew Salkey in 1977:

> We have to engage as we did in CAM and we become vulnerable to each other. Because of the religious background of most people it becomes a kind of religious transformation, though most people would scarcely describe it that way. Ideological conviction is harboured at a deep level of belief and communion. That's why the squabbles appear so vicious. It's the core of a man [...] which is at stake. (7.1.77, JLR to AS, LRA/01/0698/1 Pt 2)

Building the catalogue of a 'publishing maisonette'
La Rose was already working on a never-published anthology of Caribbean poetry when New Beacon Books (first known as New Beacon Publications) began. He was an avid reader and writer of poetry. In London, La Rose was connected to events in the British literary scene partly through Sarah White's father, Eric Walter White, Literature Director of the Arts Council from 1966 to 1971. Though New Beacon did not benefit from any grants and La Rose was adamant that they maintain professional distance, his early steps into publishing were shaped by the poetry pamphlets he encountered at the Whites' family home and informal conversations with emerging literary figures, including the young Ted Hughes, in that setting. Hughes

wrote to La Rose praising an early New Beacon publication and offering some advice:

> I have at last had time to read the exceedingly interesting pamphlet TRADITION AND THE WEST INDIAN NOVEL. It made me wonder how your publishing venture is going, and how much of a chance it would have of developing into an outlet in England for West Indian Writers. Do you ever think of doing limited and signed editions—-that seems to be the way to flourish, as a small publisher, if the thing can be made attractive to collectors, as a special, numbered series. Are your own poems printed yet? (18.12.66 TH to JLR, LRA/01/0395)

Sarah White recalls La Rose's encounters with the productions of small poetry presses in London: 'I think John had in his mind to publish his poetry from way back, but looking at these booklets, seeing possibilities, he wanted something well done' (Interview). Her father had formed the Poetry Book Society and was well connected with such publishers in London, many of whom were supported by the Arts Council. The couple gleaned this emphasis on quality and sought out one of these same printers: John Sankey of Villiers Press, based in Tufnell Park. Sankey's press was part of the avant-garde City Lights movement in California, for whom he had printed works by Lawrence Ferlinghetti and an early edition of *Howl* by Allen Ginsberg. Sankey also printed books for Bogle L'Ouverture and Allison & Busby

The logistics of publishing were explained to La Rose and White by a family friend, James MacGibbon, then of MacGibbon & Kee publishing. Described in an obituary as 'a romantic communist and first publisher of Solzhenitsyn; dandy, ardent sailor, a terrific charmer with a serious interest in labour history' (Webb, WE, *The Guardian*, 4 March 2000), MacGibbon's authors included Doris Lessing and Witold Gombrowicz. Sarah White recalls:

I always remember James sitting us down in a pub in Covent Garden, and on the back of an envelope saying, you know, what the percentages are, you know, so much for royalties, so much for discounts, so much for printing costs, your unit costs, and then the rest is profit if you manage to sell enough! I remember him saying 'you're not going to make any money, but you might enjoy yourselves'. (Interview)

New Beacon always provided contracts and ensured royalties were paid annually to authors (or, as was often the case, off-set against book purchases). This knowledge was in turn shared by John La Rose with other publishers, such as Bogle L'Ouverture in Britain and Savacou in the Caribbean.

New Beacon's catalogue began with poetry and literary criticism, but its remit soon moved beyond these centres of interest that had been central to the Caribbean Artists Movement. The catalogue developed organically in the early years, reacting to some projects as they arose and fulfilling other goals envisaged from a much earlier date.

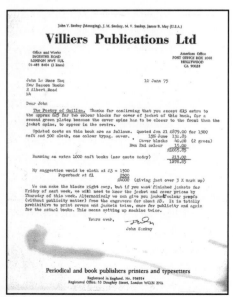

Letter to John La Rose from John Sankey of Villiers Publications.
Archive ref. GB 2904 LRA/ (uncatalogued)

Adolph Edwards' short biography of Marcus Garvey began life as a paper given at a study group organised by C.L.R. James, while a chapter from Kamau Brathwaite's PhD thesis was published in an economical paperback edition as *Folk Culture of the Slaves in Jamaica* New Beacon reprinted important early titles, such the work of nineteenth-century Trinidadian teacher and writer, John Jacob Thomas' *Theory and Practice of Creole Grammar* and *Froudacity*. La Rose also planned a reprint of *The Origins of the Taino Culture* (1935) by Sven Loven, but the project was not completed (the book was recently reprinted by the University of Alabama Press in 2010).

The early 1970s were dominated by the growth of protest and community organising activity focused in particular on discrimination against young black people by the police and in schools. New Beacon's first 'best-seller' was Bernard Coard's polemical *How the West Indian Child is made educationally sub-normal in the British school system* (1971) a publication undertaken on behalf of the Caribbean Education and Community Workers' Association (CECWA). This period also saw the founding of supplementary schools, including one in John La Rose and Sarah White's home. Some of these schools continue to exist across Britain today. The movement expanded in the mid-seventies with the founding of the Black Parents Movement and the Black Youth Movement (archives of both are housed at the George Padmore Institute). In parallel to this activity, New Beacon published more poetry: *The Pond* by Jamaican writer Mervyn Morris and *Poems of Succession* by Guyanese writer Martin Carter; a reprint of an early history of the West Indian Labour Movement by Arthur Lewis; Andrew Salkey's *Georgetown Journal*; and an introduction to the work of Nicolás Guillén by Dennis Sardinha.

New Beacon's emphasis lay on producing accessibly priced yet high-quality paperback books. A shorter run of hardbacks was produced for some books, for distribution to libraries. Most editing and proof-reading was done by John La Rose in the early years as Sarah White was completing her thesis. In later years White took on much of the proof-reading work as La Rose's commitments to other political campaigns, such as the Black Parents Movement, increased. The majority of New Beacon's early book covers were illustrated with original art by Caribbean artists Art Derry and Errol Lloyd. Their work was often abstract or not directly related to the books' content and it avoided the exoticising or stereotyping tendency visible in the packaging of earlier Caribbean writing by other publishers. New Beacon Books was concerned with opening out the notion of Caribbean and black identity by showing new possibilities and scope, rather than with creating neat packages for easy consumption.

Book distribution and the struggle for autonomy
Distribution to the Caribbean and within Britain remained a challenge, since New Beacon did not use any of the existing distribution services to get their books into bookshops. The early covers referred to the publisher as New Beacon Books: London and Port of Spain, and carried separate prices for the UK, Caribbean and the United States (sales were recorded separately for these three regions). Most publishers at this time would use an established distribution firm, but New Beacon deliberately undertook the work themselves. White recalls:

> We always wanted to control our own distribution, to know where stuff was going. It's not like we gave the distribution to someone like Turnaround or Central [...] you can obviously give your books to a distributor who will do it all for you and do all the invoicing and everything else. And we didn't really want to do that. (Interview)

In the early years, Dillons bookshop on Gower Street stocked New Beacon's books in central London, thanks to the interest of Gillian Shears who ran their Africa Department. La Rose and White abandoned WH Smith since they would only take books on a sale or return basis, meaning that unsold copies would be returned to the publisher, often in poor condition. Margaret Busby, co-founder of Allison & Busby, recalls that 'the general experience you had trying to get into the chain bookshops here was, you know, "Black people don't buy books; Black people don't read books"' ('What we leave we carry'). New Beacon's work challenged such assumptions, both through educational campaigning and their commitment to independent publishing and bookselling. Interested readers also travelled from outside London to buy books at New Beacon which they then shared with friends at home in other parts of Britain. One historian cites the example of a woman who moved to Northampton in 1973 but continued to travel to New Beacon several times a year as a means 'to support and further her development as a Caribbean and a Black person' (Watley, 232). Distributors such as Book Centre in north London, Turnaround or Third World Books in Birmingham did offer support, but New Beacon preferred to keep their distribution in-house. Many of the early publications, including *Foundations*; *Tradition, the Writer and Society*; *Creole Grammar* and *The Pond* sold out their print-runs of between 2000 and 3000 copies within a few years, reflecting keen interest in this material and the effectiveness of New Beacon's distribution network.

In the early years New Beacon informally arranged 'agents' in the Caribbean and the United States, and John La Rose also visited the Caribbean frequently to meet booksellers. This face-to-face contact was essential to ensuring the best distribution possible for New Beacon's titles. In 1976, for example, John La Rose visited the following bookshops during a trip to Trinidad: Mohammed's Bookstore, Abercromby Bookshop, Cassia House Bookshop, Stephen's Bookstore. He took lists of New Beacon's books, brought deliveries and tried to secure further orders (often for only 10 or 20 copies of each book, though some books, such as C.L.R. James' *Minty Alley*, were more in demand) (Caribbean Trips, LRA/01/0183 April – May 1976). In 1978 he was taken to visit the Tapia printworks by their founders, Lloyd Best and Allan Harris, and also travelled to bookshops, libraries and publishers in Barbados (University Bookshop, Yoruba Press), St Vincent (Mack's Bookshop, Beqiua Bookshop, Carnegie Library, Wayfarer's Bookstore) and St Lucia (Voice Bookshop, Sunshine Bookshop, Lithographic Press, Noah's Arkade). After his meeting with the manager of Yoruba Press in Barbados, he wrote in his notebook:

Yoruba Press is beginning to challenge for book publishing to be used as educational material in the Barbadian educational system. This will challenge the monopoly now held in educational publishing by Nelson, Longman, Macmillan etc (JLR notebook 4).

The question of breaking into the educational publishing market would remain elusive, however, due to the resources of smaller publishers. John La Rose made various attempts to meet representatives from the Ministries of Education to promote particular books, but with little success. Which books made it into classrooms, and how, remains an area for future research. La Rose wrote to Merle Hodge, then a tutor at the University of the West Indies, Mona expressing his awareness of this situation:

What we have never had in the Caribbean so far is a serious Education reform movement, we need to focus on the curriculum content and the examination of objectives to which that content is geared. Radicalism has always assumed that with the change in political regimes, we will get change in education. What we have got is more of the same. (17.6.71 JLR to MH, LRA/01/0386).

An expansion of a physical Caribbean branch of New Beacon Books was contemplated in the late '70s. La Rose and White registered the publishing house as a Limited Company and even found a suitable location near Oistins, Barbados, in 1979. The project did not come to fruition partly due to logistics, and partly due to the distractions of the increasing workload in London from 1979 into the early '80s with the success of Bala Usman's *For the Liberation of Nigeria* (1979) alongside La Rose's many campaigning commitments and, from 1982, the annual Book Fair.

Towards a radical black publishing space

New Beacon was always keen to encourage and offer advice to other young black publishers starting out in Britain, the Caribbean and the United States. It was never only, or even primarily, a publishing house, but was working to define an independent space for writing, reading and talking about radical black thought. In London, the most significant of the other start-ups were Bogle L'Ouverture, formed in 1968 by Jessica and Eric Huntley, and the Race Today Collective, born out of a split with the Institute of Race Relations in 1972. Allison & Busby was another key publishing house, co-founded by Margaret Busby and Clive Allison in 1967, though its list did not contain exclusively black authors. Other small publishing ventures included Karnak House (founded by Amon Saba Saakana, aka Sebastian Clarke), Karia Press (founded by Buzz Johnson), Blackbird Books (founded by Rudolph Kizerman), Black Star Publisher (Len Garrison) and Centerprise (founded in 1971 by Glenn Thompson). These various publishers worked largely in co-operation, particularly from the late 1970s onwards, following fascist attacks on several radical and black bookshops and the launch of the International Book Fair of Radical Black and Third World Books in 1982.

Bogle L'Ouverture
This London-based publishing house was founded in 1968 by Guyanese activists Eric and Jessica Huntley. It was named after Jamaican hero of the Morant Bay uprising, Paul Bogle, and Haitian revolutionary, Toussaint L'Ouverture. Its bookshop in south Ealing was renamed the Walter Rodney Bookshop in 1981.

The Huntleys migrated from Guyana to Europe in the late 1950s. They had encountered John La Rose first in the Caribbean through their involvement with the People's Progressive Party in British Guiana, now Guyana. When they met again in London, their bond was strengthened by political discussions and their shared social circle (Goulbourne, 144). The Huntleys lived with Irma and John La Rose in Uplands Road in 1964-65 and they emphasise the formative role played by John La Rose's wide knowledge of the Caribbean islands in their conversations (Alleyne, 25; Interview). The 1965 Guyana Symposium, organised by the Huntleys, debated dissatisfaction with Forbes Burnham's government, race riots in Guyana and the involvement of the US in the country. Speakers included Walter Rodney and it was during this event that the Huntleys' long friendship and strong working relationship with Rodney was cemented.

Their first publication in 1969 was a collection of papers by Rodney, *The Groundings with my Brothers*, with a cover by Errol Lloyd. This was published in response to the banning of Walter Rodney from the country by the Jamaican government in 1968. The forced exile of this rising leader and exceptional pedagogue led to riots in Jamaica, where political stagnation had set in since the independence of 1962. The Huntleys, together with lawyer Richard Small and prominent mathematician Ewart Thomas, organised a demonstration at the Jamaica Tourist Board in London in response and Jessica Huntley organised community funding to finance the publication. The autonomy of this funding initiative was crucial to the ethos of what then became Bogle L'Ouverture Publishing (Goulbourne interviews, tape 2, LMA). Eric Huntley notes the importance of publishing in transforming the status of written knowledge in the black community in Britain. This is linked to a growing awareness of the function of publishing in mediating knowledge:

> In the '70s, people didn't know what publishers did [...]. When you said that you were a publisher people looked at you: what does that mean? People in the community didn't know exactly. They knew what a printer did. Or they had an idea what a printer did. But what publishers did... (Eric Huntley, Interview)

Rodney's book set out in clear, incisive prose the major political issues faced by the region and potential political solutions, informed by his research in London and Dar-es-Salaam. As Harry Goulbourne writes: 'where many radical black Americans drew a simple line between black and white, Rodney's work hinted at a more complex situation in which racial and ethnic identities were wrapped up with the interlacing histories of a wide Atlantic world' (147).

Bogle L'Ouverture turned to John Sankey to print Rodney's essays as a stapled book. They had originally planned a pamphlet run off on the Gestetner duplicating machine, as was common in left-wing campaigning groups. It was Jessica Huntley's idea to publish the book, as Eric Huntley acknowledges:

All credit to her, she realised that as usually certain types of work is given over to women and she would have had to type the stencils and it was a messy affair, so Jessica decided, 'Let's print it'. And hence the printer came into it, rather than doing it on a Gestetner. (Interview)

There were both practical reasons and symbolic reasons for publishing this book, which was then sold or given away in order to raise consciousness of the situation in Jamaica. John La Rose offered further support when the Huntleys moved to Ealing and in 1972 set up their own bookshop in their front room. He lent stock and gave advice, as Jessica Huntley recalled:

John was very instructive: get a book and see what we like about the book, he would say. And I've heard myself telling people who want to publish what they can do. See if they like that particular style of the book and so on. (Interview)

In its early years, Bogle L'Ouverture was a less planned enterprise than New Beacon's long-term gestation. The Huntleys were from a different social milieu and had not played an active role in the CAM movement. Nonetheless

Cover of Bogle L'Ouverture pamphlet.
Archive ref:
GB 2904 LRA/01/0698/1

they were close to many CAM members, in particular Andrew Salkey and Errol Lloyd, and recall sharing discussions of the novels of Sam Selvon, George Lamming and V.S. Naipaul. They published children's books (a series of three books by Bernard and Phyllis Coard was planned, though only the first one, *Getting to Know Ourselves*, was produced), poetry (by Linton Kwesi Johnson, Lemn Sissay, Valerie Bloom), and Walter Rodney's seminal work, *How Europe Underdeveloped Africa* (1972; joint publication with Tanzania Publishing House), which has since sold over 100,000 copies. The Huntleys faced some early accusations of dividing the community by creating a rival bookshop and publisher to New Beacon: criticisms which both John La Rose and the Huntleys repeatedly refuted. The Huntleys' valuable archive is housed at the London Metropolitan Archive (LMA) and testifies to the role of publishing within their activism (Andrews, 2014). An annual Huntley conference is also held at the LMA, organised by the Friends of Eric and Jessica Huntley.

Race Today

The Race Today Collective was formed in 1973 as part of a break with its founding body, the Institute of Race Relations (IRR). John La Rose was an important sounding-board that year, given his own role as chair of the reformed IRR and friendship with its newly elected director, Ambalavaner Sivanandan. The Institute of Race Relations had been founded in 1958 to research international race relations as part of a liberal shift in post-war understanding of race. It published reports on the Notting Hill Riots of 1958 and other studies, including a controversial study of race in Britain, *Colour and Citizenship* by E.R.B. 'Jim' Rose. By the late sixties, it was increasingly criticised by its more radical followers who were sceptical of its close connections to the state and its other funding sources

Race Today October 1978.
Archive ref.
GB 2904 JOU/1/1/87

(including the Ford Foundation) and an apparent lack of impartiality in its research. In pursuit of a more radical confrontation with issues of racism in British society, Race Today broke away to form an independent body based in Brixton, while the IRR continued to carry out significant research and published the journal *Race and Class* under its new leadership.

The Race Today Collective included journalist and broadcaster Darcus Howe, writer Farrukh Dhondy and poet and activist Linton Kwesi Johnson. Together they published the important radical magazine *Race Today* (1973-1988), edited by Howe, which contained articles on radical anti-racist political activities, campaigns and cultural events in Britain and internationally Its staff included David Clark, Leila Hassan (subsequently editor), Nancy Dodge, Lorine Burt, Hilary Arnott and the graphic designer Julian Stapleton (who also designed books and illustrated covers for NBB). Prior to the break, the IRR had run a successful series of publications in partnership with Oxford University Press, but this programme ceased in 1973.

Race Today published sixteen books between 1977 and 1988, beginning with a pamphlet by Darcus Howe, edited by Sarah White, entitled *The Road make to walk on carnival day : the battle for the West Indian Carnival in Britain*. The collective subsequently published poetry, non-fiction and fiction by authors including Linton Kwesi Johnson, C.L.R. James and Jean 'Binta' Breeze.

Allison & Busby

Allison & Busby was founded in 1967 by Margaret Busby and Clive Allison. Busby was born in Ghana, of Trinidadian heritage. She met Clive Allison while studying at the University of London, leading to a successful business partnership. They published several poetry volumes on a part-time basis before committing themselves full-time to the publishing house from 1969. Busby describes their lack of knowhow in the early days:

> We thought, everybody's doing slim hardback volumes of poetry, so we're going to do cheap paperbacks – so we printed 15,000 paperback poetry books, and with no distribution. Our distribution was stopping people in the street and saying, 'do you want to buy a poetry book?' (Interview)

Their breakthrough book was Sam Greenlee's *The Spook Who Sat by the Door* (1969) which was turned into a successful film and remains in print today. It was printed by John Sankey at Villiers Press, while Busby herself made the cover, using Letraset transfers.

Allison & Busby benefited from widespread press coverage and were soon receiving up to fifty typescripts a week. This meant they straddled the parallel publishing circuits: sympathising with independents, such as New Beacon and Bogle L'Ouverture, and exploiting the strategies of the mainstream publishers. Though Busby has a long-standing interest in black literature, having

Sam Greenlee (standing) at the West Indian Students Centre. *Archive ref. GB 2904 LRA/5 (uncatalogued)*

published Buchi Emecheta, Nuruddin Farah and C.L.R. James, she has also resisted the company being labelled a 'black publisher' (Interview). She was not actively involved in CAM, nor with the political activism of the Black Parents Movement, but made a strong contribution to the Book Fairs and shared her broad experience with new publishers. She has campaigned for diversity in publishing since leaving Allison & Busby in 1987 (when it was bought out by Richard Branson's W.H. Allen imprint) with initiatives such as GAP (Greater Access to Publishing), co-founded with Jessica Huntley. She continues to play an active role in promoting African and Caribbean writing, through her writing, consulting work, journalism and work with various literary prizes (including *Wasafiri* magazine, the Caine Prize, the SI Leeds Literary Prize and the Etisalat Prize in Nigeria).

Bookshop Joint Action
Bogle L'Ouverture, Race Today and New Beacon worked together on two major projects in the late 1970s and early

Bookshop Joint Action.
Archive ref. GB 2904
BPM 6/1/1/6

1980s: the Bookshop Joint Action Committee and the International Book Fair of Radical Black and Third World Books. The first of these was an organised response to a series of fascist attacks on minority-interest independent bookshops that took place between 1977 and 1979 against a context of wider social unrest and racial intolerance that characterised those years in Britain. Ranging from arson to graffiti to threatening letters, bookshops across London and subsequently in Birmingham, Bradford, Leeds were subject to various forms of violence and intimidation. The Bookshop Joint Action Committee was formed in response. It organised press releases, campaigned against the inadequate response of the police and provided support during this difficult period. These events are fully documented in the archives of the George Padmore Institute and the Huntley Collection at the London Metropolitan Archives.

Unpublished manuscripts at New Beacon Books
Together with its concrete achievements, the New Beacon publishing archive contains the trailing threads of many partly completed or imagined book projects: the seeds of ideas, unpublished manuscripts, planned publications. These incomplete projects tell us much about the

development of New Beacon's work and the practical obstacles to building a publishing catalogue. According to the radical left-wing French publisher, François Maspero, what a publisher does not publish is often as important as what he or she does (Hage). With this in mind, New Beacon's boxes of unpublished manuscripts are an important, if largely invisible, element of their publishing history. Of these several hundred manuscripts some are long forgotten, while others, including work by Anthony McNeill and Jan Carew, went on to be published elsewhere. The list reveals that La Rose planned at least three series: a Black Power series called 'Black Star' which would include speeches by Stokely Carmichael and an interview with Huey Newton published in *Ramparts* in September 1967 (Black Liberation file, unpublished manuscripts); a Lost Literature series that would include *Minty Alley* by C.L.R. James and *Pigments* by Léon Gontran Damas (5.4.67 KR to JLR, LMA/01/0698); and a series of short histories and biographies focused on Jamaica (Johnston, LMA/01/0440). That New Beacon received so many manuscripts from across America, Africa and Europe is further testament to its visible success in forging a new independent space in the landscape of British publishing.

One manuscript, dated 1974, is the typescript for a new volume of poetry by Sierra Leonian writer Syl Cheney Coker. This volume, 'The Graveyard also has teeth' was eventually published elsewhere, but the letters reveal the author's process of revising the poems against his increasingly acrid sense of political corruption in Sierra Leone. Coker's connection to La Rose is significant. One poem, 'To a tormented playright', dedicated to Sierra Leonian dramatist and director, Yulisa Amadu Maddy, lists cases of oppression faced by writers. It poignantly acknowledges the shelter La Rose provided:

Remember, I said, how furious I was
that Vallejo had starved to death in Paris
that Rabearivelo had hanged himself
suffocated by an imaginary France
and I introduced Néruda and Guillén to you
and how in desperation we sought solace in the house
of John La Rose that courageous Trinidadian poet!

A neglected aspect of New Beacon's publishing work is its efforts to build connections beyond the English-speaking world. This work between languages and colonial contexts was seen by La Rose and White, and by the participants in CAM, as a key aspect of their activism. They sought to build a wider regional knowledge of Spanish and French Caribbean literary culture, publishing an introduction to the poetry of Nicolás Guillén and making various attempts to publish translations of francophone literature of the Caribbean and lusophone writing from Brazil.

The archives contain unpublished translations of Aimé Césaire's *Cahier d'un Retour au Pays Natal* and *Discours sur le Colonialisme* (translations by St Lucian author, Jacques Compton), both published in new editions by Présence Africaine in the 1950s. These translations built on the successful performance of Césaire's *Cahier* organised by John La Rose for CAM in 1969, though they were never actually published. Indeed, Gordon Rohlehr wrote to La Rose in 1969 expressing his need for the text: 'I am very anxious to receive a copy of your translation of Césaire's *Cahier*. Very anxious indeed. I have been planning to do a translation for my own benefit, but what with *MOKO* & lecturing, I haven't had the time' (21.7 No year, GR to JLR, LRA/01/0684/2). The first published translation in English, by John Berger and Anna Bostock, appeared in 1969 published by Penguin. New Beacon also planned to publish June Henfrey's thesis on Aimé Césaire (LRA/01/0379, LRA/01/0183), though the project did not come to fruition.

As in Britain, the situation for publishing Caribbean literature in French was dominated in the post-war period by publishers based in the metropolitan capital. Présence Africaine, the ground-breaking journal founded in 1947, and its publishing house, founded in Paris in 1949, was the symbolic hub for black writers and artists in the francophone world. John La Rose admired the work of its founder, Senegalese intellectual, Alioune Diop. Although they worked in a very different historical and national context, Présence Africaine played a similarly instrumental role in opening up new possibilities in the French book market for writing by black authors (Mudimbe; Salgas). Alioune Diop had strong links with the earlier *négritude* movement and maintained connections with the Senegalese poet and later President, Léopold Sédar Senghor, in particular through his role in co-organising the 1966 Festival of Negro Arts in Dakar. By the late sixties, Senghor's dream of *négritude* as a practical political ideology was seen as outdated by many, in particular by young anglophone African intellectuals.

In November 1968, Wilson Harris wrote to La Rose:

> There are interesting articles though I must confess I have many reservations [...]Now in the so-called Third World there is a new fashion – an African package [...] if I were asked to trace something in the history of man which corresponds to freedom or revolution I could only find it in certain 'enigmatic' works of sensibility – enigmatic because they refuse to be packaged and therefore they [play] witness to the profound 'dispossession' of man. (WH to JLR 10.11.68, NBB/1/3)

This interesting passage reflects Harris' aversion to any contained or homogenous notion of 'Africa' and his desire to step outside any overbearing categorisation when it came to imaginative work.

There is more extensive archived correspondence at the George Padmore Institute regarding a possible publication of Léon Gontran Damas' poetry by New Beacon in the early '70s which includes a signed agreement with Présence Africaine releasing the rights for his fiercely-voiced collection *Pigments* (1937). This volume had been banned in francophone Africa during the war, perceived as a threat to the loyalty of French African troops to the French army. Its first English translation was by the Trinidadian writer and academic Merle Hodge (author of *Crick, Crack Monkey*) who had completed a dissertation on *négritude* writing and also gave a talk on Damas for CAM in 1969. Merle Hodge's unpublished preface to the translation recuperates the value of Damas' work at a universal level. She is alert to accusations of essentialism faced by *négritude* writing in the English-speaking context after the euphoria of the independences and concludes:

> One must beware of seeking to force the whole of *Pigments* into the frame of Negritude or racial revolt. One out of four of these poems is inspired by the themes which inspire all poets – night, war, dreams, woman, the passage of time – there is for example the touchingly beautiful poem 'Regard' where Damas steps out of his skin as it were and contemplates with a wistful smile the old age that befalls all men. (Preface, p7, unpublished manuscript)

The CAM newsletters contained extracts from Merle Hodge's presentation and translations of several of Damas' poems. Yet the complete translation did not appear: a translation was published elsewhere and the project seems to have broken down over questions of rights. La Rose described this wrangling over rights as a 'very unnecessarily difficult nonsense' (5.4.73 JLR to Merle Hodge, LRA/01/0386).

In the same period, La Rose pursued the project of publishing work by Brazilian playwright Abdias do Nascimento which explored links between Yoruba culture and Brazil. This followed the success of Nascimento's production of his play *Sortilege* with the Black Experimental Theatre Troupe at the 1966 Dakar Festival of Negro Arts, a landmark event organised by now-President, Senghor, and the founder of Présence Africaine, Alioune Diop. Over the next decade, La Rose sent Nascimento books concerning political activity in Portuguese-speaking Africa and suggested edits for the translation of *Sortilege* by Peter Lownds. Nascimento sent photographs and paintings to be used in the publication (21.1.75 AdN to JLR, unpublished manuscripts file), but the project appears to have foundered at that point. The play eventually appeared in 1978 with Third World Press in Chicago, the largest independent black publisher in the United States, founded in 1967.

Hispanic traces in the archive include correspondence with Roberto Marquez, an editor of the *Massachusetts Review* with whom La Rose made contact via Brathwaite in April 1973. La Rose planned to publish poetry by Pedro

Perez Sarduy and essays by Rogelio Martinez Fure, whom he had met during an informal meeting in Havana during the 1967 Cultural Congress (Walmsley, 138). As the campaigning work around the Black Parents Movement took off, there were only limited resources to pursue translation projects. Nonetheless, these are some of the frequent signs of imagined possibilities at New Beacon, which expand the horizons of an emerging radical publishing space.

Aftermaths and futures: still dreaming to change the world
The 1980s were a boom period for New Beacon. They published important books by significant authors, including Roxy Harris, Lorna Goodison, Erna Brodber and Ngugi wa Thiong'o. During this period, John La Rose was closely involved with the New Cross Massacre Action Committee, the International Book Fair of Radical Black and Third World Books, and the Committee for the Release of Political Prisoners in Kenya. As a result he was increasingly distant from the day-to-day running of New Beacon Books, which continued to depend on the commitment of its staff, Sarah White, Michael La Rose and Janice Durham, and a circle of friends and volunteers (7.11.78, JLR to AS, LRA/01/0698/1 Pt2). New Beacon's publishing work has diminished in the 1990s and 2000s and now faces an uncertain future. The physical space of the bookshop continues to inspire those who visit it, yet Sarah White notes judiciously:

> John said [...] in a letter to Kamau about the ending of CAM — that organisations flourish, flower, they belong to a certain time, and then they die, and to be quite honest I think we have to begin to think about, you know, how does one come to, as it were, a successful ending, probably.

The thriving work of the George Padmore Institute will certainly be part of such a transition. The work of New Beacon's sister organisation has gone from strength to strength since its launch in 1992. This archive, education and resource centre was first envisaged as the John Jacob Thomas Institute by John La Rose over forty years ago. As he described the project in a letter to Brathwaite:

I want to set up a John Jacob Thomas Institute of Afro American Studies, which will function around a complete collection of Caribbeana, as well as the Afro Americana which we will be collecting. As you already know my Afro Americana will not be confined to the United States, but will include the whole of the American continent. All this has to do with my ideas concerning the demystification of the word in publishing, the pursuit of the creative principle within mass conceptions which are so dominant, and demand uniformity all the time, and also the idea of not accepting inhibiting traditions, but being constantly inventive and novel. (24.2.69 JLR to EKB, LRA/01/0143/4)

A planning meeting was held in May 1970, to which Andrew Salkey, Ewart Thomas, Waveney Bushell, Ralston Nelson, Susan Craig and Stuart Hall were invited (JLR to SC, 14.4.70, LRA/01/0242/2). Built on the same ethos of independence and located above the New Beacon bookshop in north London, the Institute maintains a dedicated space for meetings and book launches and for studying the many branches of black radical activism.

Though family-run firms once formed the core of British publishing, the industry has become increasingly corporate in the late twentieth and early twenty-first centuries and is now dominated by a handful of international companies who have bought out smaller publishers and are able to cater to the global marketplace (Thompson, 2010). The merger of Penguin and Random House in 2013, for example, has left them in control of 25% of the world's book market. Many independent publishers and bookshops face uncertain futures. Unable to compete on traditional terms, they must find new strategies for attracting authors and marketing their books. This project does not extend to the thorough research that remains to be done on the radical black publishing space from the 1980s to the present day (Squires, 2012). That work would analyse the impact of the corporatisation of publishing and the digital revolution on radical black publishers and the status of politicised art in a global literary marketplace. In turn it may assess and explore the current need for independent publishing spaces. Building on the work of the GAP programme and Independent Black Publishers, which campaigned for adequate representation of BME groups in publishing in the 1980s and 1990s, such research might continue to map the sociology of the publishing industry. It could explore the extent to which the acclaimed 'bibliodiversity' of the English-language book market (excluding its paltry proportion of translated books) is supported by an adequately diverse pool of editors and thereby develop a qualitative response to 'In Full Colour', the first survey on Cultural Diversity in Publishing, carried out by the Arts Council and *The Bookseller* in 2004 (see also, Kean, 2015, a follow-up report on the limited diversity in UK publishing, released after this essay was first published).

The archived correspondence at the GPI, much of which is handwritten on thin blue airmail paper, tracks the development of ideas between La Rose, White and their many interlocutors across America, Europe and Africa. The letters frame an intricate network of personal and professional relationships. With this network in mind, the question must be raised of what it means for New Beacon, as for Bogle L'Ouverture, to encourage work in its archive. Who is that archive for? When, why and how will its contents be used? How does the archival urge to record the past work forward towards a productive idea of continuity as advocated by La Rose? What does it mean to 'dream to change the world' in 2013, as opposed to 1967 or 1951, when Martin Carter first wrote that line in his stirring poem 'Looking at your hands'? The work of New Beacon and other radical black publishers was motivated not by the commodification of art nor of cultural difference but by a powerful sense of political and social purpose. The role played by these 'publishing maisonettes' was shaped by constant communication and contact with individuals and institutions in the Caribbean throughout the late 1960s and 1970s. New Beacon's publishing work can be seen both as a continuity of Trinidadian intellectual tradition and as the expression and catalyst of a key period in the history of radical black politics in Britain.

This brief history re-affirms that creative ideas expressed in writing are always mediated by institutional contexts and the political, cultural, social and economic structures which surround them. The always contingent question of change leads us to ask now what can be learnt from the work of New Beacon at a time where traditional publishing is undergoing such rapid transformation. Might the digital platform offer the autonomy and freedom they have advocated for so long? How are the human relationships at the core of New Beacon's work transformed in this new setting? How to define and achieve freedom of written expression is a more relevant question than ever in the age of digital print. Understanding the relationship between writing, reading and political activism remains vital on both a local and global scale.

Bibliography and sources

Interviews with Sarah White (27.3.13), Jessica and Eric Huntley (11.4.13), Anne Walmsley (11.4.13), Errol Lloyd (18.7.13) and Margaret Busby (24.7.13). 'What we leave we carry' BBC Radio 4 documentary on John La Rose and New Beacon Books (broadcast 11 January 2011), edited by Burt Caesar.

'Dream to Change the World' film on the life and work of John La Rose (2003), directed by Horace Ové.

Adim-Ado, Joan. *Longest Journey. A History of Black Lewisham*. London: Deptford Forum Publishing, 1995.

Alleyne, Brian. *Radicals against race: black activism and cultural politics*. Oxford: Berg, 2002.

Andrews, Margaret. *Doing nothing is not an option: The Radical Lives of Eric and Jessica Huntley.* Middlesex: Krik Krak, 2014.

Athill, Diana. *Stet: a memoir.* London: Granta, 2000.

Beezmohun, Sharmilla. 'Bridging the Gap: The International Book Fair of Radical Black and Third World Books (1982-95)'.

Bradley, Sue. *The British Book Trade: An Oral History.* London: The British Library, 2008.

Busby, Margaret. 'John La Rose: obituary' *Wasafiri* 21.3, 2006, 65-67.

—. 'Writing the Wrongs: 50 years of Radical Black Publishing in Britain'. Unpublished keynote address given at Huntley Archives Conference, London Metropolitan Archives, Saturday 17 February 2007.

Currey, James. *Africa Writes Back: The African Writers Series and the Launch of African Literature.* Oxford: James Currey, 2008.

Davis, Caroline. *Creating Postcolonial Literature: African writers and British publishers.* Basingstoke: Palgrave Macmillan, 2013.

Frioux-Salgas, Sarah, ed. 'Présence Africaine' Special issue of *Gradhiva* 10, 2009.

Fryer, Peter. *Staying Power. The History of Black People in Britain.* London: Pluto Press, 1984.

Goulbourne, Harry. *Caribbean transnational experience.* London: Pluto Press; Kingston: Arawak, 2002.

Hage, Julien. 'Une brève histoire des librairies et des éditions Maspero 1955-1982.' *François Maspero et les paysages humains.* Eds. Hage, Julien et al. Lyon: La fosse aux ours; A plus d'un titre, 2009: 93-160.

John, Gus. 'La Rose, John Anthony (1927–2006)'. *Oxford Dictionary of National Biography,* Oxford: Oxford University Press, Jan 2010; online edn, Jan 2011 [accessed 30 July 2013]

John La Rose Tribute Committee. *Foundations of a Movement.* A Tribute to John La Rose on the occasion of the 10th International Book Fair of Radical Black & Third World Books. London: John La Rose Tribute Committee, 1991.

Johnson, Linton Kwesi. 'Obituaries – John La Rose'. *The Guardian,* 4 March 2006.

Kean, Danuta (ed.). Writing the Future: Black and Asian Writers and Publishers in the UK Market Place. Spread the Word, 2015. Available at:

https://www.spreadtheword.org.uk/resources/view/writing-the-future [consulted 9 October 2016].

Low, Gail. *Publishing the postcolonial: anglophone West African and Caribbean writing in the UK, 1948-1968*. London: Routledge, 2011.

McKenzie, D.F. *Bibliography and the sociology of texts*. Cambridge: CUP, 1999.

Moore, Gerald. 'Transcription Centre in the Sixties: Navigating in Narrow Seas'. *Research in African Literatures* 33.3, 2002, 167-181.

Mudimbé, V.Y., ed. *The Surreptitious Speech: Presence Africaine and the Politics of Otherness, 1947–1987*. Chicago: University of Chicago Press, 1992.

Phillips, Caryl. *Colour me English*. London: Harvill Secker, 2011.

Phillips, Mike and Trevor Phillips. *Windrush: The irresistible rise of multi-racial Britain*. London: HarperCollins Publishers, 1998.

Sivanandan, Ambalavaner. *Race and Resistance: The IRR Story*. London: Race Today Publications, 1974.

Squires, C. 'Too Much Rushdie, not enough Romance?: The UK Publishing Industy and BME (Black Minority Ethnic) Readership'. In: Procter, J., Benwell, B., Robinson, G. (ed.). *Postcolonial Audiences: Readers, Viewers, Reception*. Abingdon: Routledge, 2012, 99-111.

Thompson, John. *Merchants of Culture: The Publishing Business in the Twenty-First Century*. Cambridge: Polity Press, 2010.

Watley, G. *Identity and consumption practices of Northamptonshire Caribbeans c.1955-1989*. Doctoral thesis. The University of Northampton. 2012.

Walmsley, Anne. *The Caribbean Artists Movement 1966-1972*. London: New Beacon, 1992.

White, Sarah, Roxy Harris and Sharmilla Beezmohun, eds. *A Meeting of the Continents: the International Book Fair of Radical Black and Third World Books – revisited: history, memories, organisation and programmes 1982-1995*. London: New Beacon Books, 2005.

Surge

JAY BERNARD

Surge and/or Silence? an Introduction

A message of hope and contradiction
But such is my message.

— John La Rose

We don't let go of each other easily and that is the seed of
our freedom.

— Karina Ray

The title of this sequence, *Surge*, comes from a 1983 panel featuring Darcus Howe, CLR James, Sonia Sanchez and Ngũgĩ wa Thiong'o, entitled 'Resurgence or Barbarism?' Like us, they were in a contradictory moment: a rise in black activism and organisation was coupled with a very active and hostile political right. The two sides fed each other, and the left was eventually able to put its fascist opponents on the back foot, if not extinguish them completely. But Darcus Howe made a very interesting point: 'When you surge and you don't deal with the question, barbarism expresses itself... When you surge, you have to have a definite political conclusion, otherwise you dip again.' In a video recorded on the night of the Black People's Day of Action two years before, he is seen in woolly hat and coat, breath rising in the freezing air, expressing what that conclusion might be:

> Freedom now. Freedom from all oppression. Freedom from petty discrimination and petty thugging whites. Freedom from the fear of manipulation by governments, that we carry on with us — freedom from all that, so that we could be ourselves and contribute to this country... what a lot of you don't know that we have to contribute.

We are currently experiencing a disorienting resurgence of black activism and a slide towards fascism. What we are facing is both the same ugliness that characterised the 1970s and 1980s, and a completely different beast. The rhetoric used by black radicals thirty-five years ago no longer works to undermine a political right that has adapted to new economic and technological conditions. The tone has shifted. The bandwidth for ideas has been massively increased by social media; the language of hate is more slippery and opaque; the populist cry to tear up the rule book and bring down the elites is an ingenious concoction of radical capitalism, paranoid survivalism, economic grievances, exhilarating populism and breath-taking political gumption.

My three month residency at the George Padmore Institute began shortly after Brexit and ended just before the election of Donald Trump as president of the United States. I often felt that the documents from thirty or forty years ago, that I was reading, could be describing the political situation today. So it was understandable that many people reacted to Brexit and Trump by saying that this was the same old shit: racism, classism, sexism, imperialism. They'd seen it all before. But this actually strikes me as an incredibly reckless position because it reduces the tenets of this new right-wing assertiveness to what we know already – what we have *diagnosed* in the body politic. But perhaps the resemblance of our current leftist discourse to that of the late twentieth century is a cause for alarm; perhaps it suggests stagnation and might be a clue as to why the right has found its feet again.

Howe's call for a definite political conclusion feels important, but I wonder if there's an equal need for the deliberate renewal of that political conclusion, and that currently this renewal is only ever in the face of a crisis. I think of the Armistice Day fireworks that recently went off in central London: the same gunpowder that took the lives of those we are meant to mourn is also what creates this celebratory spectacle. It's the same stuff, but different. The temptation to say that this political climate is the same as it has always been denies the differences – and those differences have given rise to a new political power. I am black, queer, and as wedded to the –isms of the twentieth century as anyone else, but I sense these terms losing their descriptive powers, because they no longer accurately invoke the knot of current social and political relations. Racism, sexism, classism – the words that have dominated leftist critique in the run up to Brexit and Trump – may not be the best words in the best order. They might be starting to resemble the term 'racialism', a primitive word that fell out of favour and was replaced by 'racism' which is basically the same idea. But the right have built up a resistance to being called racists, and even learned to diagnose it in others for their own gain: think Ken Livingstone. So we are facing an adjectival crisis, as much as anything else. How do we speak? And from what position? And how can we ensure that we are heard not only by those who oppose us, but by our allies, who are also lost for words?

I wanted to concentrate on the New Cross Massacre because, as we celebrate New Beacon Books 50th anniversary and the George Padmore Institutes twenty-five years of making things audible and known, it is a piece of history characterised by silence. The New Cross Massacre Action Committee (NCMAC) was formed to protest the muffling of the case by the police, the silence of the media, and the silence of Margaret Thatcher and the

Queen (neither of whom wrote letters of condolence to the families of the New Cross victims until forced, five weeks later.) The testimonies of many of the survivors were retracted having been given under duress, and the forensics implied that the fire started in the middle of the living room – which, according to many, was empty. A strange white man was reported to have thrown something at the house then sped away; an incendiary device was found below the window, and the police were silent about it so that only themselves and the perpetrator would know of its existence. Close inspection of the records shows that the details of a 'carpenter' – a white man with the same profession as Christ – are missing, despite a lengthy (and strange) interview with the police. It's hard to tell, but it looks like the details have been tippex'd out. A violent apparition haunts the case, and what is terrifying is that the culprit – if indeed there is one – might have been among the party goers, or in the street walking that cold January morning. They might have met eyes with Mrs. Ruddock as she screamed for her children – she reported men in their shirt sleeves watching the fire, saying nothing and doing nothing to help.

If there isn't a culprit, then the chilling nature of the case remains: my interest in the New Cross Massacre was stoked partly because it remains a testament to the attitudes of the state towards marginal people – it demonstrates in a nutshell how silence is used to intimidate and obfuscate. The total indifference with which the news was met was compounded by the reluctance of the state to investigate members of the fascist parties that operated in the area. Lewisham was the HQ of many right-wing groups and there had been concerted efforts to shut down black parties, which were deemed loud, disruptive, and dens of illegal drug and alcohol sales. The sound of black people was posed as an existential threat. If you were up until 5am, listening to blue beat, you couldn't possibly be employed, family-oriented or of good moral character. Reading the interviews conducted by both the police and the NCMAC, it is clear that many young people were targeted, pressured and forced into confessions by the police, one of whom openly says, 'Black people are liars', and that a great silence was maintained because racism – an extremely useful social tool – is perpetuated by denial.

What is less public is the manner in which those confessions came about. In one set of interviews in particular, a boy accuses another of providing a knife for the 'fight' that supposedly took place in the living room. He ends up accusing someone who died in the house of starting the fire, and even the police officer interrogating him is taken aback by the perversity of the claim. One parent describes the interview questions presented to him by officers as 'so low' that neither officer could look him in the eye. An interview with the youngest person to survive, an eleven year-old girl, is filled with silence. The transcripts mark her out as so obviously a child unable to respond to the pressure she detects but cannot understand, particularly when she complains to her father that her words have been twisted. She says 'Yes' at one point, which the officer takes as a confirmation of his assertion that there had been trouble at the party – but she was in fact trying to confirm that she had answered a previous question in the negative. Still another document features a hastily hand-written conversation among unrelated notes: it appears to be an overheard conversation between two officers, in which one complains about being on the case twenty-four seven and being 'fed up'; his interlocutor points out that Column 88 probably did it to which the exasperated officer replies, 'That's bullshit.' One reporter, who attended the funerals of the thirteen dead children and was part of the media silence around the case said she did not write about it because 'nothing happened'. John La Rose's handwriting is often present in the margins questioning the testimonies given and trying to piece the facts together. He is all over the testimony given by the aforementioned 'carpenter', and seeing his many exclamation marks and heavy underlining at the same points I detected as spurious, felt as though he was re-reading it through my eyes.

The presence of voices in the absence of justice is what drives the poems in *Surge*. Taking a cue from Marlon James's *A Brief History of Seven Killings* – a novel that is entirely the voices of its characters – and Marlon Riggs's practice of combining poetry and documentary, I decided to write from the position of those whose voices we cannot hear, namely the young people who died in the fire. But I also wanted to explore the fact that these were ordinary people, with ordinary families that loved them. These were kids who formed collective sound systems, who negotiated relationships among themselves in mature and open-minded ways, who developed a culture and a language that echoes in England and in English today, who went out on the streets in the face of incredible hostility and were *joyous* about it – they kept carnival going, they fought the sus laws that would attempt to intimidate them, they continued to throw parties and organise among themselves, and they continued to demand space in every area of British public life. I wanted to explore the aftermath of the fire – the silence, the separation, the charred remains, the loss and the mystery of what happened in those early hours on January 18th 1981. I also wanted to create something protean, mutable, never-ending – a kind of conversation I could keep having with myself about who I am and who I speak to. The poems contained in this book are the beginning of what I hope will be a longer project.

Brexit, in particular, affected the direction this residency took, and has made me question some of the delusions that characterise the left: our tendency to believe that we pose some sort of threat. But Brexit showed how psychologically dependent we are on the EU (which is a racist, neo-imperialist entity) and our entitlement to freedom within it, even if we can understand how the referendum was used to manipulate the public. It is a strange feeling indeed, to be on the left, and to have the sense that somehow we have been outdone and are unable to comprehend the fizzing lingo, energy and vision of people who are, without question, nostalgic for a more hostile time. I am not a politician, I have not studied politics, I am (like almost everyone else) largely ignorant about how the law actually works. But I am here, and I am listening to people speak, and the resounding note in this political climate is the ineffectiveness of once powerful terms and the concurrent death of empathy, which, as Hannah Arendt has written 'is one of the earliest and most telling signs of a culture about to fall into barbarism'. And there are signs aplenty.

The lip-service recently paid to the historic struggles of black people by Theresa May at the Tory party conference is a sticking plaster. It falls to the floor. She has happily departed on the right-wing bandwagon that drives through the night leaving figurative burning crosses on the lawns of migrants, Muslims, citizens from other EU countries, and the class of black and Asian people whose roots in this country are already two and three generations deep. These crosses are the front pages of the *Daily Mail* and *Daily Express*; vans telling migrants to GO HOME or face arrest; parents being asked to provide proof of their children's citizenship; total inaction in the face of the migrant crisis; not a single police officer convicted for a custodial death since 1990; unprecedented levels of surveillance granted by the Investigatory Powers Act; the continued bombing of other countries; and the very concrete message that the climate that created the New Cross Massacre is not a passing historical feature, but a deliberate social policy – a tool that political elites are well aware is at their disposal.

To borrow from Sara Ahmed: at the moment, the destruction of empathy is figured as the love of one's country. To speak empathetically is to betray the nation; to present the 'foreign born' or 'foreign looking' or 'foreign sounding' person as worthy of love is to undermine the tacit acceptance of white English supremacy, and its predication on the oppression of others. If we say it aloud, we cannot help but hear that it is wrong; to make that utterance is to undermine those who have invested their political hopes in it – they want a better future for their children, never mind the children of others. Indeed fuck the children of others who would take the bread and meat and jobs and houses of you and yours.

So this is the voice I use in the poems. Simple declarations of love and personhood, by those who perished – the children of migrants, some migrants themselves – most feeling deeply the pain of their parents, siblings and friends. In a joyless twist of fate, as I was finishing this introduction and tweaking the final draft of *Surge*, I found myself in the toilet on a plane to Nairobi, suddenly aware of a man screaming. I went out and saw that he was a young black guy handcuffed to his seat, surrounded by four enormous white men. Trying to understand what was going on was no use – it stalled take off, and they simply called security and threatened to throw me off. But what struck me was the fact that nobody else on the plane, including someone I happened to know as an activist, said or did anything. The passenger next to me turned and said, 'Hopefully he'll shut up.' And indeed he did. The handcuffed man was silent all the way.

Jay Bernard
November 2016

Surge

1

I was so weak, I was sickened,
I was grieved, I was sad,
I was everything that's bad –

    my voice became the glass
        breaking in the heat

    I was so sickened and so grieved

    I was so weak – I called
and no-one seemed to call with me
no-one seemed to know or see
    what I had seen –

    I was so sickened and so grieved

and I said to the child I knew
    harboured in the fire – jump

Yvonne, jump Paul, jump –

    I said, I called – jump

Yvonne, jump Paul, jump –

my voice it was so weak

    – Paul, jump –

so sickened and so grieved

2

Me seh ah two step fahwahd an ah two step back
Me seh ah tree step fahwahd an ah six step back
Me seh ah four step fahwahd an ah one step back
Me seh ah one half fahwahd an ah one half back

Me seh ah left side fahwahd an me right side back
Bust up left side right side haffi change tack
    Me seh half de revalushun deh pun de attack
    Only half a salushun to de tings dem we lack

Me seh gyal love reggae an gyal love move
Bwoy love reggae an im love up im groove
    Di two ah dem rub up an starting to move
    Crowd gone quiet, people stop nyam dem food

An dem watch and dem see this wicked emcee
This beautiful gyal all dress up in green
    Nails done nice, hair cris, wha yuh mean
    Di baddest likkle gyal dem evah did see

Me seh ah two step fahwahd an ah two step back
Me seh ah tree step fahwahd an ah six step back
Me seh ah four step fahwahd an ah one step back
Me seh ah one half fahwahd an ah one half back

Me seh di heat ah di night ah come up thru di floor
Black smoke ah rise tho dem nevah did know
    Di music ah jam an di young man ah chat
    Word fly from him lip like vampire bat

An di gyal dem ah dance an di man dem ah rock
Drink six rum an black an di beat dem ah drop
    Darkness descend and di room gone black
    Voices ah call seh dem haffi get out

Voices ah call seh dem haffi get out
Screamin begin an di people ah shout
    Me seh screamin begin an di people ah shout
    Dem ah covah dem head an ah covah dem mouth

Me seh ah two step fahwahd an ah two step back
Me seh ah tree step fahwahd an ah six step back
Me seh ah four step fahwahd an ah one step back
Me seh ah one half fahwahd an ah one half back

Down pun di street yuh see body face down
Pickney fly thru di air an mash up pun di ground
    Flames dem ah fly an ah furious red
    Bwoy fall from di window an yuh know seh him dead

Gyal fall back inside an we no see her no more
No bright green dress up pon di third floor
    Police man come an fireman too
    Dem startle dem scared an no know wha fi do

Mudda she ah cry an she nah have no shoes
Man dem ah look but to help dem refuse
    Fren dem shock by di scale ah di loss
    Black smoke ah billow down there in New Cross

Me seh black smoke ah billow at di house in New Cross
Me seh black smoke ah billow at di house in New Cross
Me seh blood ah goh run for di pain of di loss
Me seh black smoke ah billow at di house in New Cross

Me seh ah left side fahwahd an me right side back
Bust up left side right side haffi change tack
Me seh half de revalushun deh pun de attack
Only half a salushun to de tings dem we lack

Me seh ah two step fahwahd an ah two step back
Me seh ah tree step fahwahd an ah six step back
Me seh ah four step fahwahd an ah one step back
Me seh ah one half fahwahd an ah one half back

3

When they lifted me my neck snapped
and my head landed cheek down
I saw the officer's foot jump back
his hands shook as he wiped the soot
I noticed the rudded gold of his watch
how pink his nails gleamed through the gloves
the white-gold ring like sausage string
on a near translucent finger
He paused and seemed to see me watch
him searching for a gaze to meet
He darted out his hand and grabbed my
head and dropped it in a plastic bag
I glimpsed myself beside the bed
saw for a second my stiff black hands
no nails or thumb or life line left
no heart tattoo or amber palm

-

the room was black the sky was black
the smoke came through and breathed us in
the house we knew the friends we left
up they went dust again
I heard they found that boy you liked
but couldn't say if it was him
until they locked his mother's door
with a key found winking in the ash

-

They put me on a table beside my photograph
a rubbish one that showed all my spots
They blew it up so it was just my face
But remember you were there to the right
and remember how that afternoon we
put our fists together and checked
who was dark and who was light
I was the darker one and wondered
why it was I was not like you
Why I hadn't been born browner or white
When it did not seem that hard to do

4

Blank was loved by all, loved more now that –

It wasn't Blank's fault that they grew up in a –

My sister went to school with Blank and said that they were –

Blank had been lying face down when the ambulance –

No-one recognised the body, there wasn't anything to –

Blank was loved by everyone, they were always gonna –

Blank ran in to save his friend when suddenly –

Their daughters were inside, watching from the window –

It gets tiring, it gets boring, forgive me, it's hard to understand –

Several thousand people marched in the rain from –

And now what is there, Blank? What do we have to show for –

Did we fail? Did we do too little? Is it something you or I –

How are you baby? It's so good to hear you, so good to hear your –

I didn't know you were in trouble. I didn't know you were in –

I'm sorry, I don't know anything about that. I can't help you –

And I read that you were loved Blank, and you were always
        gonna –

The family of Blank today issued this statement –

It is thirty five years since the death of Blank, what have we
learned from –

Blank broke their own neck in the back of the –

The officers involved have defended their actions and been
given –

How are you babes? I just wanted to call. To talk. To tell you –

I read that you were loved, I read that you were –

5

The light that evening changed
from white to blue shot
with siren blue
the heat and rain
co-steam in green and grey
The flash of the photographer
leaves hot white
wherever the world looks:

they twist back her arm
handcuff her and lift her to her feet
pull back her snarling face for the press

We watch

The many seeing and the seen
spread through the park near
Speaker's Corner, buttoned up
their feet wet through and cold,
all huddled and brave
and cold, and there together,
departing to the sound of the last rasta
distant through the megaphone.

Oh Jah. Oh Jah.
Every lord called upon,
every church song sung,
every psalm and saying,
every aunt chasing duppy from the living room
cannot bring us back,
nor the speakers, nor the bass,

nor the sound system,
nor the hooded spectre of police
nor the cold wide park where
everyone leaves us,
moves on home,
Not knowing we were there
marching too,
Not one staying long enough
for us to savour.

6

E

Then the officer said to me that they heard something about you, that you were missing because you didn't want to face the facts, and I said well why not make you tell the truth – and don't torture you. And the officer looked at me. He really looked at me as if to say I was a liar too. But he didn't say anything. He put his hands behind his back and he walked to the window. Outside I do a lot of gardening. And he said he liked my garden. And the other officer said we don't know where your son is. I said how can you not know, aren't you the police? He said we don't know everything, if we did we'd have solved this bloody – and the officer by the window turned to look at him, and he didn't finish his sentence. Two days later, they came back and asked whether I had heard from you. I said no. He asked whether I recognised any of the following objects. A yellow shirt. A piece of brown trouser leg. The sole of a shoe. And a penny piece. I said you had been wearing a yellow shirt, and you loved your brown corduroy trousers. And they said well this is all we have left. Last he took out a silver key, and I knew immediately it was yours. I knew it would go straight into that front door. I asked them for your body. And they said they didn't advise it, me going to see what was left. So I sat down on the sofa, and I have been talking to you and only you since.

O

The officer said that it's very common for culprits to go
missing. I said my son isn't a culprit, and how dare he imply it
when you doing so well in school. One of the officer stand up
by the window and look out and is making all these
comments. He didn't want to look us full in the eye. He make
it clear from the moment he step in the house what he think of
us. Anyway we offered them a cup of tea. And then they come
back a few days later – I think the Tuesday – and they said
what you was wearing on the night of the fire? I said probably
your new trousers. And he said was you wearing a yellow
shirt? I said yes. Brown shoes? I said yes. And he took out the
items from one plastic bag, and he says does this look like it
belong to you? I says yes. And he says do you recognise this
key? I said why don't we try it. We had to wriggle it, but it fit.
And he says, I'm sorry. So I said what are you sorry for? I want
to see my son. Them start stammer. Them say them don't
think it is a good idea. I said, I am your father, I want to see
you. So I went down with two friends – Marcia did drive me –
and them lead us down to a room and on the table there you
was. No face, nothing to speak of. I said, this is the body where
you find the clothes? Them nod. So I said, it must be you. This
must be my son.

I am glad you came, dad, I had been lying there all day, and I couldn't move. I opened my eyes and I was in the house and everything was black, dad. I had been at the party a few hours and I didn't know anything about what happened. And I felt someone touch me, but I was stiff. I never been so stiff before. And I tried to say it's me, it's me, who are you? But they were looking at me so strangely, like he couldn't stand to look at me, dad. Police always looked at me like that. And he turned me over, and he took the shirt from under me, and I said that's my shirt, but he didn't hear me. They wrapped me in a blanket and drove me here, and I was lying there waiting for you, dad. Across the table, there were bodies, dad. Twisted like nothing I've ever seen. No heads. Feet like a mummy's. Horrible figurines. There were loads of them, I swear, all lined up and police came and looked at them, like in a museum. And then they were looking at me, and I heard them say my stomach had burst, and I thought I hadn't eaten at all that day. They looked at my teeth. Someone put a cold metal thing in my mouth to scrape and it was like water, that cold was so good against my lips. And then you came and I was calling out to you, dad – and I know you heard me because here we are. Come back. Don't bury me. I know that's what you're gonna do. But I can't stand it. I can barely stand it when the lights go off and I'm here and spend the whole night listening. I want to crawl between mum and you in your bed, in your sheets. That's the only kind of burying I want.

7

I'm in my cousin's pocket! And he took me upstairs
To play scalextric, and he said can you sit on the car
I said probably and he laughed because he said my
Voice was different, so squeaky. I said who are you
Calling a girl and he said he would crush me like a
Man, like He-Man would crush his opponents, so I
Said all right and he sellotaped me down to the car
And pressed the controller and round I went like I
Was in Miami, and the sun was on me and I was a
Famous actor and all the girls loved me and I was
Smoking the best grass ever made from Kingston and
High as the canopies in National Geographic, I was
Like woooooo! Woooooo! Wooooooo! And the car was
Like eeeeeeeehhhhh! Ehhhhhhhh! And my cousin
Was like can it go faster? I said don't break it! And he
Went faster, and then he said is it normal for boys
To cry? And I said why you getting deep for I'm at 100
Miles an hour here! Started shouting fish finger fanny!
Sherbert cigarettes! Thatcher Thatcher Thatcher,
Oi oi oi! Flying Saucer! Rob that ugly bitch! Did you
Know cuz there's a hole at the end of your dick
And if you're careful you can put things in it! Wooo!
He bent down and stopped the car and looked at me
And tried to put a massive finger on my head, I said oi!
Batty boy! Don't touch! But he didn't laugh. First time
he's done that. Looked at me and walked away.

8

will anybody speak of this
the way the flowers do,
the way the common speaks
of the fearless dying leaves?

9

I went back to my mother's kitchen: Peas was soaking on the stove and a lettuce was uncurling on the counter. A blue plastic bag filled with fish was deflating. One of the eyes was pressed against the side of the bag and seemed to be the only one that noticed me. This kitchen:

the crack in the window; the spice rack with over a hundred tiny bottles; outside, my brother's underwear on the line – tiny boxer shorts in the drizzle; the fridge with a poster for bonfire night just gone, and a postcard from our aunty in Antigua, and a vase of plastic flowers on top – ultra-violet blue yellow purple making the green of the leaves seem quite improbable; beside it a small shelf peopled by Erna Brodber, Gus John; the door to the bathroom:

I know that the floor is cold; there are three coiled hairs in the sink; a streak of toothpaste where my brother spits and never washes it out; I know that the toilet seat is cracked; I know what it's like to come in here when it's dark outside and turn the taps and feel the whole house warming up; the gradual breath the house takes through the wallpaper, the carpet, the timber, the kettle, the dutch pot, the kippers sparking in oil, the television, the toaster, the paraffin heater, and the first ray unencumbered by the clouds that spreads its rose palm on the kitchen window:

I will be that for my brother and mother. I will be light touching their faces as she guts the fish, drains the peas.

10

yes – i come here when i was six – many years now –
i was a likkle cricket fan in short trousers
        and i love my mother –
she was my grandmother –
        i never knew my mum til i come here –
and she raised me with my three sisters
        who treat me very well indeed,
because i was the smallest and the last
to come to england, and when i arrived i knew
        something had happened to me,
i knew that what i saw in the mirror had been
        recontoured and differently arranged –
when i looked at myself in my new tie and shoes i saw
something like a net that catches death, i thought:
        here i am, six years old
and already i feel like my life is finished,
        nothing left –
i was with two strangers, my mother and father,
who bathed me and it felt like two ghosts
        rubbing soap on my shoulders –
two dead people in their house clothes
telling me to wash my neck –

and i thought: here i am six years old
        and i feel like i have to hold on,
else i do as i did when i stood up
        on the window sill in my briefs
and i look down and i said god, i said,
        i don't want to die in this country,
i said let me die with my grandmother –
i want to be rotted by the sun,

and i want her shadow to fall along my body
and i want to be shaded by her grief,
and i want the dogs in the yard
to scratch their heads indifferent,
i want to be eaten by worms and
            become an ackee tree, lord, i said –
i said it in such a whisper
            i could have put the ground to sleep:
don't let me die in england i said to the pavement
            and the shining black rain upon it –
and never tell my grandmother
            why I never called to say that
i thought of her daily,
            or why i never said much in christmas cards,
or thank her on the phone for all that was freely given –

many nights before this one i wondered
            what she thought of that,
what she thought of the littlest grandchild
who couldn't say that
            many nights before this one
i tried to forget that i loved her,
turned the pain of her remembrance
to the bitter lie that she could not
have loved one such as me
            and the proof was in the distance –